I dedicate this photo essay to the memory of my father and his love of the ocean.

Finding

NEWPORT BEACH ■

A Photo Essay

Kate Houlihan

Finding

FOREWORD ■

For almost five generations my family has lived, worked and vacationed along the coast of California. I treasure my memories of visiting relatives and listening to stories about the good old days in California, "… when the surf was big, and the land was aplenty." My relatives witnessed – and helped – the Golden State grow, and lived through turbulent times. They were bankers who survived the Great Depression, civil engineers who helped build Ventura County, and ranchers who grew avocados and citrus for two major produce companies in California.

As a child I remember how my parents loved our west coast beaches, and passed this love on to us. My dad told of his adventures bodysurfing at the Wedge, or sailing to Catalina and the Channel Islands with his cousins. He and my mom shared their mutual respect for the ocean with our family by treating us to summer vacations up and down the California coast. We rented cozy beach cottages, played in the ocean, and tried every water sport possible including fishing, bodysurfing, Boogie boarding, and surfing. Each town we visited had its own unique culture, landmarks, and way of life. Somehow these towns have held on to their personalities, and if you look through my lens you will see the characteristics that make these beach communities distinctive.

Newport Beach has a variety of characteristics that make this community exceptional, such as its energetic surf culture, the charming town on Balboa Island, and the unspoiled vistas of Crystal Cove. The locals say the weather is comparable to that of the Canary Islands; as far as beauty, Newport ranks among the top places in the world. Although the city was incorporated in 1906, it feels new. It is sprinkled with glam and glitter. Yet, as you see by my photographs, Newport still holds on to its roots – honoring them, and treasuring them, just as I treasure mine.

Finding

RECREATIONAL HARBOR ■

Newport Beach has a complex history behind its evolution from a port-side, commercial town in the early 1800's, to a destination city with a bustling recreational harbor. In order for this transformation to have occurred, major dredging and changes were required to make the harbor and the bay safe to navigate. By 1936, through policies and funding from private investors and the government, the final dredging was completed, jetties were constructed, and the beginning of a recreational harbor and bay was underway.

Newport Harbor now boasts more pleasure craft than any west coast harbor, with some of the oldest private yacht clubs in the country. The recreational

harbor attracts visitors and residents with boat shows, sailing and seamanship programs, regattas, fishing excursions and the spirited Newport Harbor Christmas Boat Parade. A variety of boats surround the seven small residential islands in the harbor, including the largest, Balboa Island, which was created as a result of the dredging process.

Connected to the harbor is the Upper Newport Bay, or "Back Bay." The bay is popular for kayaking, canoeing, and rowing. A first-class rowing training facility draws the attention of recruiters from colleges across the country.

As a protected ecological reserve, the Back Bay is known for two hundred species of migratory and local birds.

The surrounding trail is used for hiking, bicycling and horseback riding. Many of Newport's first influential people did not agree on a vision for the area – originally desiring a commercial port or a resort town with a European feel. Regardless, I'm sure they would be pleased to find what Newport Harbor has become today: a recreational harbor that never sleeps.

DORY
FISHING FLEET
FOUNDED 1891

DORYMEN'S
FISH + CRAB
FRESH DAILY
FROM THE SEA

Finding

CRYSTAL COVE STATE PARK ■
HISTORIC DISTRICT

The southernmost border of Newport Beach is Crystal Cove State Park. Consisting of over three miles of pristine beaches, wooded canyons, and elevated vistas, Crystal Cove is a gem. Long before it became a state park, Crystal Cove played a part in the lives of early native American Indians, farmers and ranchers, and even Hollywood producers in search of a desert island setting. As early as the 1920's vacationers visited this secluded beach to escape the hustle and bustle of the city, and over time, a small community developed. Simple cottages were built on leased land. Eventually the land was

sold to the State Parks and the beach dwellings were to become a five-star resort. However, locals resisted. Through the efforts of preservation groups such as Crystal Cove Alliance, the cottages and beach front where saved.

Crystal Cove's trails, pristine beaches and Historic District continue to draw people: the youngest explorer hoping to get a glimpse of a sea anemone in the tidepools; the plein air artist anticipating a rich golden sunset; or the family searching for a beach-side vacation that takes them back in time.

Finding

BALBOA ISLAND & THE BALBOA PENINSULA ■

Sheltered by the safety of Newport Harbor, Balboa Island could be its own little country surrounded by a moat, and ruled by a king and queen. There is a bond between the villagers on the Island; it is as if they speak their own language. The island streets are lined with quaint cottages (some circa 1930) and contemporary remodels. A favorite pastime for health-conscious and canine-loving Newporters is to "walk the Island," especially during the holidays. Whimsical decorations and outlandish displays make it fun for the entire family to view as they stroll along the strand, or from aboard one of Newport's own electric Duffy boats, while cruising the harbor. During the weekend of the Newport Harbor Christmas Boat Parade, this area is a wonderland of splendor.

Since 1911, visitors and locals have used a ferryboat to cross the harbor from Balboa Island to the Peninsula, docking at the famed Balboa Village area and Fun Zone. Still today, visitors ride the Ferris wheel, shop, and sign up for fishing trips and excursions to Catalina Island. During the summer, Junior Lifeguards can be seen on the ferry, bound for the lifeguard headquarters where they report for the rigorous training program on the beach.

The Balboa Village area, which once felt like a seaside carnival, is now comprised of a smaller assortment of shops and restaurants, the Newport Harbor Nautical Museum, and the Balboa Pavilion. The Pavilion has a rich history, and has drawn many visitors over the years. It was a popular destination for the many forms of entertainment it provided, including art exhibits, concerts, dancing, bowling, and gambling. In 1963 the Pavilion was dressed up with 1500 light bulbs, making this historic building one of the most recognized landmarks on the Balboa Peninsula.

Finding

SURF CULTURE ■

Nothing says Southern California more than surfing…although Polynesians and the Hawaiians may disagree with this statement. After all, they developed the sport and brought it to California. It was no accident that the surf culture took hold here. Newport's community organizers cleverly promoted surfing events in order to draw more people to the sport and thus to local beaches. In the early 1900's the city organized surfing demonstrations and lessons with George Freeth, one of the "Fathers of Modern Surfing," as well as famous Waikiki surfer and Olympic Gold medalist in swimming, Duke Paoa. It wasn't long before Newport Beach became known as a surfing town with some of the best surfing breaks in the world. Whether it is Blackies or the Wedge, there are waves, tides and swells for every type of surfer, from weekend warriors to dawn patrollers.

Finding

THE WEDGE ■

I grew up in the 1960's hearing about the incredible bodysurfing at "The Wedge," a famous spot where my dad and his buddies would head for a little "body slamming." My dad preferred bodysurfing because he didn't need a board of any type, and could just "hit the waves" anytime. It wasn't until I was older that I realized how dangerous this famous place could be.

The Wedge is a well-known surfing location where the jetty at the opening of the harbor meets the tip of the Balboa Peninsula. The incoming swells bounce off the jetty and the refraction causes a "wedge effect," sometimes resulting in waves up to thirty feet high. On big days like this, it is difficult to find a spot on the beach because people gather 'round trying

to get a glimpse of the enormous waves and the daring surfers.

The Wedge has become a sacred place for bodysurfers, especially a group of locals who refer to themselves as the Wedge Preservation Society, or Wedge Crew. These are experienced athletes, some of whom have been bodysurfing the Wedge for 40 years. Because this area can get so crazy when shared among bodysurfers, skimboarders and bodyboarders, the Crew successfully petitioned the city for preset blackball hours which disallow boards of any kind. When the lifeguards raise the yellow blackball flag, bodysurfers rule the Wedge.

The distinctive wave patterns and size of the breaks at the Wedge have made Newport Beach internationally known as having one of the most exciting bodysurfing spots in the world.

Finding

THE WOODIE STATION WAGON ■

One of the iconic symbols of a beach town is the classic "woodie" station wagon. (Can't you just hear the Beach Boys tunes coming from the car now?) Originally used as taxis, station wagons became popular for personal use, especially for surfers needing to transport their surfboards – and their friends' boards – to the beach. Driving up and down the coast you can still spot a few of these classic cars today – particularly if members of the local Woodie club are meeting nearby. Some local buses have the wood-grain look, too…reminding us of the surfing culture that continues to be so much a part of Newport Beach.

photo index COVER ▪ Three surfers heading out at Blackies Beach | DEDICATION ▪ Bluff restoration by the river jetty, north end of Newport Beach TABLE OF CONTENTS ▪ Crystal Cove State Park with Catalina in the distance | FOREWORD ▪ Beach at the Wedge, looking north | 4 ▪ Lifeguard tower at the river jetty separating Newport and Huntington | 5 ▪ Seal sculpture by Kay Finch looking out by Inspiration Point in Corona Del Mar | 7 ▪ The infamous Blackie's Bar | 8 ▪ Little Corona Beach looking south toward Laguna | 10 ▪ View from under Newport Pier | 11 ▪ Newport Pier | 21 ▪ Girl walking on bluff at north end of Newport, by river jetty | 24 ▪ Woody's on the Peninsula and Newport Burger on PCH | 25 ▪ Balboa Boat Yard and Crab Cooker (est. 1951) on Balboa Peninsula | 26-27 ▪ Entrance to Newport Harbor from bluff above Big Corona Beach | 29 ▪ Dorymen's fish market by Newport Pier | 31 ▪ Pearsons Port, a fish market below PCH across from Bayside Drive | 32 ▪ The famous electric Duffy boats, originally from Newport Beach, found throughout the harbor 34 ▪ Outrigger canoes at the Newport Aquatic Center, on the Back Bay | 35 ▪ Crew team practicing on the Back Bay | 39 ▪ The Historic Balboa Pavilion 42-43 ▪ Boats with Holiday lights for the annual Christmas Boat Parade | 46-47 ▪ Cottages at Crystal Cove State Park | 51 ▪ Tunnel under PCH leading to Crystal Cove State Park | 52 ▪ "Fun Zone" on Balboa Peninsula | 54 ▪ The infamous "Balboa Bar," ice cream dipped in chocolate, rolled in nuts, a must! 55 ▪ Dad's Snack Bar on Balboa Island | 56-61 ▪ In and around Balboa Island | 63 ▪ View looking south from 54th Street | 66 ▪ Surfing, Blackies Beach 70 ▪ Snack shack on strand down from Newport Pier | 74 ▪ Just entering "The Green Room," 54th Street | 77 ▪ Andrew Doheny cuttin' it up | 84 ▪ Junior lifeguards training on Balboa Peninsula | 85 ▪ Lifeguard tower at the Wedge | 97 ▪ Newport Harbor from the bluff from Castaways Park

information ▪ www.balboapavilion.com ▪ www.calparks.org ▪ www.crystalcovebeachcottages.org ▪ www.nationalwoodieclub.com ▪ http://newportbay.org ▪ www.ocregister.com ▪ www.stationwagon.com

© 2011 by Kate Houlihan/Naeco Publishing ▪ All rights reserved.
Photographer and Creative Director, Kate Houlihan.
Sales and Distribution, Suzanna Richter
Design and Layout, Denise Wada
Written by Sarah Drislane
Published by Naeco Publishing
Contact 949-322-2577 or http://katehoulihan.com
Printed in China through Four Colour Print Group, Louisville, Kentucky
ISBN 978-0-615-45829-8